AF284506

Joyce Shintani

BECOMINGS

joyce@joyceshintani.com

Collection curated by James Laval

Cover design by Christian Bär
www.lektorat-baer.de

Designs courtesy of
Tatiana Vásquez Arellano
www.holamiraestudio.cl

Publication by Lektorat Bär
www.lektorat-baer.de, Stuttgart, Germany

Printed and published by:
BoD - Books on Demand, Norderstedt

ISBN 9783753498928

Becomings

Joyce Shintani

Poems

Volume 2

1985 – 2021

Foreword

I am delighted to have become acquainted with Joyce Shintani's writing and to have the opportunity to curate this body of her poetry. In *Becomings*, written from 1985-2021, Shintani's central concerns are on full display: questions concerning identity, spirituality, creativity, and art. The collection reflects a lifetime of self-examination and experimentation. In these poems and fragments, Shintani explores how the self (and our multiple "selves") creates and shapes itself through art, while also being shaped and created by the world. This is a collection as much about self-exploration and self-expression as it is about the material conditions of Los Angeles, Stuttgart, and Paris, the locations where these poems were written and that influenced Shintani as a writer.

If Shintani's first collection, *Words I Couldn't Stop*, is characterized by an outward opening—emotional, creative, expressive—this collection instead occupies the space left by that opening. This void manifests itself in the poems in *Becomings* as an underlying awareness of the mortality, of the transience, and the uncertainty of the world. The comfort of religion, and accompanying pastoral tones found in *Words I Couldn't Stop* give way here to a secular, analytical, corporeal view of the world. In this collection, poetic forms are openly acknowledged as being molded, fused, and sculpted into existence, at times investigated, and rejected; just as in life the self, too, constructs, experiments, and rejects personas. Taking its cue from the collection's opening poem's first line—"I live a birth pang / who's pushing?", the constellations that structure this collection mark this formation and formulation over the course of a lifetime. I hope that others will find the same honesty and vulnerability and courage I so admire in Shintani's writing.

James Laval
London, May 2021

Preface

The aim of this and the preceding volume is not to present 'my great poems', for many are not poems at all. They are documents of 'becoming'. The writings, most in verse, tell 'herstory': the story of a woman trying to become a conductor during a time and in a place where that was almost impossible; the story of a dissociative trying to self-diagnose her disorder—just as impossible; the story of an ethnic woman—a foreigner—trying to find her identity and a place in late 20th century Europe.

Some of the poems may be good, just as some of the concerts I conducted were good. Other concerts and other poems may be of questionable value. Their justification lies not in being fine polished results to be put on display. Rather, they are signposts in a search. They document the sweat behind the performance, the paths not taken, the things left out because 'they didn't make the grade'. They are artifacts of becoming.

I am indebted to Christian Bär for encouraging and assisting me in publishing these poems at a moment in my life when nothing at all seemed possible. James Laval solved with elegance the arduous task of grouping the convolute of poems written during half a century into narrative constellations that help the reader grasp their interconnection. Dr. Dorothée Leidig never failed to share her unvarnished criticism and loving lessons with me. Finally, I thank the close friends and doctors who have made such efforts to cheer me on in a pandemic time that is dark for all.

Joyce Shintani
Stuttgart, April 2021

1 Glint in the Jet

Reaching

I live a birth pang—
who 's pushing?

High-pressure
ear-popping push,
head-splitting rush.
I ache an echo,
swim in a vacuum.

Underwater, images float past.
I'd look,
instead count seconds
till the surface breaks again.

Golden mirror mosaic
underside of heaven
bursts on brushing
into infinity fragments.
Splintered glass colors spin
in centrifugal circles—
universe in genesis.

Floating precision
airless perfection
a world from space perceived,
spied from wild bird's eye.
Wings flap noiselessly:

Antarctic to Tropic—
a lifetime journey—
yearly.

The present rushes by in plashes,
rain on a bullet's hull,
the minutes—drops of shattered time.

Before I glimpse
last rainbow flash
I pray I'll seize that prismic tune
glowing and tingling like a sparkler.

Autotoxin

Tonight the hole crawled up to my
clear-aired mountain top
and spat me in the eye.
The hole
where I'm naked,
the void of a thousand eyes straining
toward my coverlessness:
the fear that strips
every shred
of reason,
the peeling
sucking
caw
of tremulant
poison
panic,
that wipes my marrow
off its lips,
pauses,
then sucks anew.

A cavernous anthropophagus
    with a past-filled
    gas bladder—
fumes rising and stinging,
touching isolated
burned out instants

that leave scars but
don't sizzle.
To hairs on his dusty black hide
cling scabs of older hurts
whose blood is now
just a crust.
It's his mouth
     watering
for my round belly
for my soft nipple—
     offering and hopeful
     tilting upward to shiny dew apple.

I'm told I should strike this
omnivorous gape.
I should, soft and naked, pink and smiling,
swing the iron, begin the endless
leaden chain that blinds
then subdues.

I reach for the shaft to heave the blow:
Skin on shaft melds
then separates from flesh,
my hands show sinew and bone
blooding feely,
and I wonder,
where's the strength
to go on?

Solitary Abode

My foot trod
    on a snow crunch,
nose inhaled
    air that etched;
glass moon rays glazed
    whitening brightness
on fields and fields
    of blanket snow.

I took the road
    long and windless
feeling a carving cleanness
    clear my image
paring to a core
    of ache.

Alone I knocked
    on heart's door–unopened…
From the craving inner flower flowed–
    in a small silent stream–
    the serum of want.

I mounted stairs
    to my sky hole,
a payload
    of unvoiced words
    slowed my step;

I stood with my self
    at the door to my chamber
shaking with the searing search
    of need:
        soft replies,
        pillows of flesh
        and warm bone;
remember with a jolt
    who waits eternally
    alone, gentle,
    hanging head, low eyes
    in blanched cheeks
    whose last Gift
    of tender Infinity
    He's saved
    for me
    tonight;
cross the threshold,
breathe quiet relief,
lay my head
    upon his chest
and cradled, lone,
    fall to sleep.

This given me.

Contact

Pain forcing through
a melody misunderstood—
vibrates in harmony prime.

The lone vibration distills nectar
eked out in droplets
once red, thick, refined—
pure as God's purpose.

To toast this cognac
assume position
on the black plateau.

The chasm's lip,
finely limned,
cuts face and hands
of those who dare.

Down you look
past nebulae—
there is no thump,
nothing reaches bottom.

Perforations,
suns and stars,
glint in the jet—
so clear they scratch the eye.

Pose yourself,
noiseless storm behind,
wind on lashes,
raise high the glass—
a prick, a point
ignites spheric harmony.

This is air
and this is drink.

Downy Dreams

Fathers' iron
lies in us,
cold steel.
Diamond edges
bore
in the ground
of hope.

Who mined it?
Who smelted?
Their loss
whets the blade
of our resignation.

What hands
hammered the anvil
forging our will?

Hard the shoulders
and raspy the hair,
the vessels empty
of warm fluid.

But tomorrow's radiance
sprouts
in the night.

Whisper-blanket midnight,
wrap our wounds,
use us rags
to clear your slate,

and from your palette
re-color the canvas
with children's
downy dreams.

Recognition

Small being,
my light,
stood before the keys,
its task.

Never joyful
it hung its head
and its wings drooped.

Child drone
who working forgets
how to light the sparkling yes.

This poor one–
I couldn't perceive her.
She sighed.

I looked in the pit
I looked at the linen
I looked in the kitchen and
I tried in the pit
I tried in the veil
tried anonymity.

I tried with a man
and tried with a girl,
tried high mountains alone.

Asked wisest men
in my world
for a clue to this ill.

But best of all cures
I only held up,
never slipped
into the garment.

Till years
brought an answer to tears:
take time,
liberate the reins,
breathe best air,
follow your path.

2 Blasts Forth Blinding

Fire Fighting

twisted torments
finding fire that
wrestles coal
spins webs.
caught up tight
holding bonds
steel stomach

iron will vs.
iron want
hammering
welding
melding
molding
age fears
too late to start

inner hot
burning out
spilling forth
burning rim
meteor
blasts forth blinding
blots the view
observation of
vivisection

fight to find a self,
self's need
spun taut

my life in lines
life ends quick
life in a blink
fast past
document?
worth? aim?
Am I building now on stones
or on pies?
myriad subjects
await author's eye

vehicle vehement
adamant assent
querulous contention
omnivorous impotence
overflowing antecedents

flood of outcry,
though deafeningly mute

Move.

Externalizing

Trembling shaking
suspecting
sensations
possibilities

a mate cups closer
than ever before
fits so close
where only men were

A miniature sequence
shakes my world
free-seeking truth,
forming without rules—
I'm drunk with fantasy!

Quietly trace a soft man's notes
upon the printed page
seek to identify
the source of song
I feeling search
touch open wounds—
share my wounds and nerves.

But I am more than feeling friend
more than patient wife,
I need more blood, more air
insatiably

My hunger's more than
reproduction–
Give me world to eat!

Through these days I ramble
hearing a chinking new chime
I hear a voice
its name is Joyce
I'm fresh and feel this tune
My virgin pulse is hard and fast
it finally finds its team
this week I've learned my beat–
seek unspeakability.

Nocturnal

The words plop out
lumps surrounded by runny sugar water
like bad marmalade on a plate.

There's an iron wedge inside.
An anvil. It doesn't move.
It is "being in love"–
like being at the doctor's:
waiting in the waiting room
nauseous, shaky,
knowing he'll soon cut.

A love poem would like to be written–
it crouches, hunkered,
longing to find cruise level
but the whip will crack
and the shot will fly.

I am a sad, hulking owl.
Leaden my wings
and it is still day
I sleep. The heavy thing
has its prison in me.

Lurid midday sunlight
sucks the dew
off my nightly fancies.

And so we proseate,
that poem and I.

Mantra

The feet through the sand,
the wind and the waves,
the blinding white glaze of
a sun without face—

The play of the surf
caresses the mind, but
the gust in my breath from
horizons afar
grasps the air,
takes gasp from my breast—

Now past me, now toward me,
the panting fast footsteps
are chanting a yearless refrain:
"away and away and away".

Communion

The great thing that resides within
I can't find its name
I know it is a boulder
a granite clod
I know it has no color—only all of them
I know its mass but not its weight
I feel it press I know it's there
At night it comes out and lies upon my chest
satin-ceilinged sarcophagus
I want to excrete it
hack it small
pull out shards one by one
reconstruct the mammoth externally
May my house here remaining
be light and airy
filled with sweet breezes
that fondle doorway curtains
like I your golden hair
when you're my heaviest ceiling
making me
yield
to your insistence
On full occupancy
of my spaces
I open and
fill you in
then forgetting time

I low
till you
leaning pressing
find
between myself and that center spot
deeper pushing
take me
to blind nirvana.

3   Man and Woman

Elektra

Child loses father,
trembles.

Years spent
boiling questions:
What is father?
What's love?

A father's found!
who ripe and sure
offers shelter to trembling seeker.

A human father
full of faults
whose towering strengths
overweigh.

Found the father.
Tentative
and thanking
I neared.

And found another tremble
a girl once felt
in daddy's coat.
Now revived
in woman warm.

Little hand
once in his,
tiny and secure—
now seeks a man's arm
with her woman's breast
but, quivering, delays…

What is it, dad,
makes fathers fear?
What motivation drives?

Unreachable—
I'd like to touch,
bring lost chance to life
I'd bring delights and giggle some.

You father—'d have to bear
the onerous load of guiding.

Do you
hesitate
to kiss the cheek
that awaits
your sure and gentle stroke?

Papa,
where's your moral?
Is the picture clear?

Mother

What does that mother feel
sitting in her shell
peering at the bloodless landscape
of Summer's dead optimism?

What does a mother feel
who hoped for family
to fill her orphan void
and got a single rebel instead?

She bartered herself then
for companionship
and got a few more shots
of purgatory.

Discovered that a child needs time
too late,
for the child already
escaped.

In Autumn she,
who never saw trees,
opened her eyes and,
wishing for green,
coughed up dry leaves—
harbingers of the coming freeze.

The Neighbor and His Daughter

Tonight I told
my next-door neighbor
about the man today
who paid me grand compliments
by following me around—his prey.
I laughed and tried
in coarse attempt
to make sense
of nonsense.

The young daughter listened, too.

It was un-bourgeois—
he threw me out
unceremoniously
and it hurt
to know
once again
my scent
too strong for company.

Picky

Auntie dear,
Your agile hashi fingers
I always admired
select a tiny sushi morsel
without wounding a neighbor.

But when it comes to truth
I wonder…
You are at times so choosy,
take only pretty grains—
and reject honest kernels.

This Man's World
Makes Me Vomit

First I ate dinner
then dessert
then another dessert.
Then another.
And another
and another.
Then some bread
and afterward,
crackers.
I looked at the dirty dishes and left the room.

Then I tried to play piano.
Beethoven, of course,
or Wagner.

Now I lie on my stomach on my bed
and vomit.
The vomit comes out slowly
or quickly
oozes
or convulses.
It foams brown and chunky
over lips
and breasts.
It burns and stings
and sticks on everything.

It wretches up from guts' bottom
and spews across the room hitting the wall
where I can watch it drip
in inkblot forms
stinking
on the carpet.

Sisters, my unborn sisters,
I apologize
for this inarticulate spasm
of rage and pain.
Almost I blaspheme,
my dear, loved, not-yet-born ones.
Your mother lover is sick
trying to exorcize her Eumenides.

*   *   *

I touched him tender
on his tender brow
brow that good-naturedly
refused to furl
beneath crushing loads;
I touched that brow—to love it—
and he said
                    —really, innocently!—
Ah, you touch so wonderfully—
and at dinner the night before
he cut off my identity
introducing me to guests as

an American music student.

I can see he doesn't mean it,
only places unwittingly
the straws that
           break
                   my back.

Minerva! Wisdom!
Find me patience in the pit
of disappointment
in despair of dead-end streets.
Guide my faltering foot
to sure understanding,
widen windowless winces,
let blow some soft zephyr
to soothe my hot pain
my burns
my burning
send me, Lord,
           love–
                   please?

*   *   *

A woman–at all costs!–
    shouldn't be strong, but
    womanly.
That means,
    she shouldn't eat garlic,

or exercise too much,
learn too much,
or think—too much—
only enough to consider
which is better:
porkchop or sirloin tip
for his dining pleasure.
Otherwise, the female creature
cuts herself off from society whole,
must expatriate herself
to a distant Greek Island
where odes are sung to all—not half—
the human race.
How much and how long
does one small artist—
"woman artist"—
suffer
under assignment
of roles?
Does she accept or
does she break?
Or, breaking icons,
sink?
How long I thought,
"I am too dumb!"
to protect myself from truth;
for if not so dumb
as all pretend,
why are all pretending?
Who contemplates these questions

sinks beneath waves
of breathtaking
nausea.

This man's world
makes me vomit.

       *   *   *

I'm sure some plucky soul will read
and suggest heartily—
"It's not so bad, courage!
Don't let it get you down!"

Dear Madam,
Stretch your hand out here:
I'll strike it with a hammer
right there on your last two fingers.
Come back next week and place again
your soft hand here
And once more I'll raise my mallet
and hard I'll let you have it.
In 10 days you'll reappear,
the nails will still be black
and this time, instead of once
I'll hammer down twice or thrice.
I hope the spattered blood washes out
of table cloth and skirt
and in parting I shall bid you
to come again soon.

This time three weeks you wait
    the cast just removed
The skin and scars are pink
    and it would be a shame
    to make you hurt again.
But treatment is treatment
    so lay your hand back
    on the accustomed spot
and once again with joy—or not—
    I'll raise my weapon high
I'll eye the distance,
    measure weight,
    velocity and space
then down the blow
    that cracks a bone.
Perhaps you'll never write again.

Sorry, Ma'am,
    it's just the treatment
    to help you understand
that when next month
    you see a hammer
you'll inkle what I mean
    when you hear my reassuring words,
    "It's not so bad, courage!
    The world is full of hammers!"

*   *   *

An hour I've written
    in hopes I'll dream—
    I've tried to expurgate.
You've beat me, world,
    robbed my mood
    my sense of worth, my leap.
I'll bound not to bed
    rather slumping I'll recline
    in hopes that Morpheus abducts the pain
    and Lethe lets forget.

How can I re-joyce
    when a stinking world
    spits turds in my eyes?
This wrecks my sight
    ruins the view
    and makes so much work to do.
Hours and hours
    of cleaning up
    just to start anew.
Now, Lord, I've tried
    to exorcise
    without much luck, I fear.
At end I'll pray.
    For only a wonder
    could make this woman human.

Man and Woman

A woman
a man
never ceasing
satisfactions sighed,
annulled,
declined.

New beginning
tree of life
blossom bud pouts.

One man
one woman
outreaching
contradictions.
High,
bursting,
lulled,
resigned.

Foreign flicker
bloom and quiver.

New man
new woman
increasing contradictions
why dulled,

defined,
rebeginning?

One more man.
What makes each unique?
Whence each solitary hue?
Hands full kisses
sparking electrics
rainbow butterflies—
all interchangeable uniqueness.

Response: alive.

4   **Where Memory's Warm**

Magic Days

I see already:
in the future
this will be
a beautiful past.

Dearest conjurer,
magician of mood,
giver of sparkle,
my fire—
who could make me happier
than you
explaining the comparative difficulty
of Beethoven's symphonies
and advising me on orchestral repertoire?

Dear man,
you almost take me seriously.
I kiss your head,
magnificent head.
I hold this head,
large hand head
tender in my
large tender hands
and plant soft
angels' breath kisses
on your scratchy cheek.

Squinty, you sit in an outdoor café
wearing earphones
and grinding your teeth,
brown corduroy jacket
in friendly Italian winter sun.
You, broad and looming
with shuffling gait,
you with uncommon balance
and commonest coarseness,
you more than all others
teach me:
what is an artist,
what is art.
Will I ever see over your ear-tips?

Generous giver
with red sun-burnt,
soft brown hair,
wind-whipped surfer's hair,
and funny curvy fingers,
pudgy fingers,
fat, ungainly fingers
that tickle
beautiful Bach
from an untuned piano
in a crummy dressing room
in a Roman opera house
where I hang up your coat
and hide bonbons beneath your hat,
hat that got lost in the restaurant

with the journalist who joined us,
and you recounted
how we drove in your rented Mercedes
and you played the despot
with Italian drivers
and walked along
and held my hand
and reached for my hand
and cupped my hand in yours
in your pocket–
and you bossed me around
and felt obliged to have
elite soft sex
and gave and gave me
stories and ears.

Waking Up

Soft spot I seek inside
where memory's warm.
I find you and caress you,
the warmth eggs me on…

Hard through my window
Miss Blue Sun warns–
she counts today's affairs:
warm spot now–or duty?

Reluctantly, I agree.

Instants

Sun, stop!
No lower!
My skin wants
your last drops.

Cold night, don't begin,
let what today was
last a few seconds longer.

Blob on the horizon
golden orb of time:
hang there,
over that cornfield
don't slip an inch—
let what has been
not yet cease.

* * *

Precious
fearful glances
through grass and lashes
so close I could see
your eyes are green
and you wear contact lenses.

The arm that had jerked away
today didn't flinch.

Long fluttered in your chest
life,
I saw it vibrate
through your cotton t-shirt.

The small finger tip
that suddenly quivered–
you said you'd misplaced
your poise.

*   *   *

"You're the first to say that to me."

The sun burned your white face
as you tried to regain tranquility.
Horses snorted in the background
and I finally rested
having said what I wanted to hide.

Such instants!

5   A Remnant of Silk

Dual Vision

The slip's the thing—
living two lives
at once
the rubbing of realities
the skew of each second
the ouch in the knees
the pressure in the eyes.
It's the hard knot
that sitting inside
pushes me
to such hard actions.
It's anger at the world
exhaustion at the fight
and disappointment.

Something drives me,
all right,
something drives hard.
I use
passive violence.
I violate the world
through myself.

I see this,
through a thick wall
of plastic.

I am distant
I am cool
with my anger,

I am in danger.

Sugie

Did it freeze that night
lacking food and means
deciding in Wakayama Prefecture?
The only way
to redeem Nishiyama's shame
was to sell the daughter, Sugie.

Not young, thick with foreboding,
You arrive from Taisho
at a California pier
Where Yaemon Shintani,
gawky and grinning,
awaits you
impatient.

What cloth of obedience,
bound in your heart
by a silken thread of hope
to repugnance,
is reduced to fringes
as Yaemon's calloused fingers
fumble hungry in your folds?

Disappointment's sour milk
flows from your breasts,
for your first and last borns,
Maru and Hisako—girls—failures, like you.

Within the drafty shack you built
the icy wind of racism
chills Yaemon's fading illusion,
an immigrant's palmy grandeur.

How sweet is the milk of success
when Kyoshi then Juro, the doctor,
pass from your dark, woman's warmth
into the bright climate of opportunity.

With *mochi* you feed us
the rising sun's soft sweetness.
With *haji* you brand our skin
with the iron of ancestral codex.
With *wabi-sabi* pottery and stitching
you pass on Nippon's fearless rustic beauty.

Meanwhile, sharecropping
on numb knees
you bake remaining dreams
into thin brittle cakes
that crumble into dust
in Riverside's blistering strawberry patch.

You howling vent your suffering
and steel your heart to withstand
the deadening waves that wash you—
inexorable tides of defeat.
But like a breakwater you resist:
Kyoshi's death,

the camps,
Juro's insanity,
Maru's lupus,
Tare's tuberculosis,
Hisako's schizophrenia,
Joycie-chan's abuse,
Yaemon's death,
finally
Juro's self-chosen end.

Obedience supports you,
and heritage is your reserve.
But milk turns to stones
that flint angry in your eyes.
At last your fire is choked,
your face a wordless map of loss.

The Shintanis
preserve
a remnant of your silk,
and we weave
with diligence and exactitude
the fibers of your story
into the fabric of our lives
under the California sun
and here, today,
in Germany.

Zeitauswärts

Every now moment
is the jet felt tunnel.

music is past
descriptions passed tense,
so books flow backward.

a sudden mango split
in time's curtain
juices
and going in
gulping life.

Shikata-Ga-Nai

Eine Geschichte, eine *kleine* Geschichte.
Meine Geschichte. Deine Geschichte?
Ein fernes Land mit Hungersnot.
Gestern, vorgestern. Heute. Morgen?
Zu Kaisers Zeiten – Meiji Zeiten.
Shikata ga nai.

Aber in Amerika sind die Möglichkeiten
    unbegrenzt!
Ein Meiji Bauer hat Hunger und einen Traum.
Kalifornien berauscht sich mit Gold.
Yaemon und sein Traum kommen in der
    Boomtown San Francisco an.
In Kalifornien fliegen Steine und Gesetze.
Yaemon ist fremd und stumm.
Shikata ga nai.

Er kauft sich eine ‚Picture Bride'.
Auch Sugie's Familie hat Hunger.
Und zu viele Töchter.
Sugie wird verkauft.
Shikata ga nai.

Aber in Kalifornien scheint immer die Sonne.
Eine Hütte, dann ein Häuschen.
4 Kinder und ein Model T.
Gaman.

Pearl Harbor wird zerstört. Die Präsidenten
    befehlen:
Japanische Amerikaner in die Lager!
Bomben über Hiroshima und Nagasaki
    werfen!
Shikata ga nai.
Gaman.

Die Nachkriegswelt boomt und blüht.
Welcher Krieg?
Welche Lager?
Wir kaufen ein!
Wir sind happy!
(Außer den Krankheiten
und Onkel in der Klinik
und Tante… pssst!)
Uns geht's gut!

Einem Nachkriegskind in Kalifornien geht's
    nicht gut.
Es hat Not und einen Traum.
„Erforsche dich, Kind, dann wirst du
    verstehen."
In Europa gibt's Kunst und Kritik.
Dort kann man lernen.
Juni mit ihrem Gepäck kommt im Land der
    Denker an.
In der Luft fliegen Steine und Geister.
Shikata ga nai.

Juni ist fremd und stumm.
Sie baut sich ein Haus aus Erkenntnis.
Gaman.

Zurück im alten Nippon die Wirtschaft boomt
      und blüht.
Wir kaufen ein!
Wir haben Glück!
(Außer den Trostfrauen,
dem Karoshi-Tod
und den kyoiku mamas
… psst!)
Uns geht's gut!

9,0 auf der Richter-Skala
„Wir haben die Natur missachtet."
Wir beklagen uns nicht.
Shikata ga nai.

Wir werden es wieder aufbauen.
Gaman.

Denkt dran, schrieb Juni.
Shikata ga nai.
Gaman.

No Spring

On my cold
moon-dawn
balcony,
copious bird communication—
Messaien's polyglots—
and the freeway rumbles:
sub-urban Spring.

But wrapped in pain,
there is no Spring.

Boulez Demeure

A while ago,
energetic,
I practiced intensive container gardening
and raised compost worms—
red wigglers.

I read
that everything around us—
granite, plants,
and all the rest—
once passed through the digestive tract
of this ancient species.

At the hour of the wolf
they were busy,
happily munching rotting garbage
and writhing in their bin—
I could hear them!
softly crunching snow steps—
producing compost,
ecologically correct black gold
that made my garden a wonder.

Stiller,
today,
my thoughts crawl elsewhere—
back to Joseph's sad last seminar,

when he told us
about Mendelssohn,
and Levinas,
and Heidegger.
That everyone dies one death, alone.

No one can compare.
So why all the chatter?

When I conducted
Mozart
and Bruckner
and Mahler
and Pagh-Paan,
didn't I bring
through my fingertips
stars from the night
into the concert air?

Worms are memories.
On my zafu,
solo,
I am preparing.
Shall I keep crying?

When I'm in the ground
the tunes I sang
will pass through tummies
of perennial red wigglers—
just like everything else.

Mochi:
soft and sweet
the plans
the dreams
the hope.

Loss:
bitter matcha.

6 **Pebbles**

Irritating swap:
innocence for
conscience.

* * *

Where there's will
there's way.
Without, only
waif.

* * *

small beach pebble
without shape or charm,
without gleam or luster—
you make up the seashore.

* * *

I swallowed words
I held my tongue
Till I was choked and dumb.

*   *   *

I've found a way
to slip in and out
and still maintain
continuity and fidelity

7   **First Poem** (1968)

Broken Prose--OOpps!

The Sky was Blue.
My Body was Cold.
A Bird pecked at the ground
in search of a worm;
He found.

break

The street was bare
my feet froze.
and then I saw a friend
walking to the 2nd.
To dead day. .
Her birthday is in May.
(Her mother's is too.)

crass

The wind is dry and icy.....
With a song in his

heart

A young boy makes a

start

He falls.
He flails.
He fails.

The race is over,
He did not win.

Broken Prose—OOpps!

The Sky was Blue.
My Body was Cold.
A Bird pecked at the ground
in search of a worm;
He found.

break

The street was bare
my feet froze.
and then I saw a friend
walking to the End.
To dead day.
Her birthday is in May.
(Her mother's is, too.)

crack

The school is dry and icy…..
With a song in his

heart

A young boy makes a

start

He   fails.
He   flails.
He   trails.

The Song is gone,
He did not win.

I saw

        the school*

I smelled

        the grass.

I touched

        the tree.   *******

I tasted

        the cold.

I heard birds, but

        I O B S E R V E D

cold mo(u)rning

Me.

That's All.

I saw

the
school·

I smelled

the grass.

I touched

the tree.   ☆☆☆☆☆

I tasted

the cold.

I heard birds, but

I O B S E R V E D

cold mo(u)rning

life.

That's all.

NOTES

The Poem *Sugie* was written on 22 July, 2008, during my first trauma rehab; revised 28 Dec 2009.

The poem *Zeitauswärts* was written in January 2011, during a workshop with poet Jan Wagner and is meant to be accompanied by the sound clip available here: http://bit.ly/shintani_news.
The word Zeitauswärts was invented by Paul Celan and might be translated as 'time outward' or 'time outside itself'.

Explanations of the terms used in the poem *Shikata-ga-nai*, written after the Fukushima disaster in 2011, can be found here: https://en.wikipedia.org/wiki/Shikata_ga_nai and https://en.wikipedia.org/wiki/Gaman_(term).

The background for the poem *No Spring*, written in 2015, can be heard here: http://bit.ly/shintani_news.

The poem *Boulez Demeure* was written on 22 January 2016, in memoriam Pierre Boulez (26 March 1925 – 5 January 2016).

My *First Poem* was written as an assignment in Mrs. Schroeter's 11th grade English class at Woodrow Wilson High School in Long Beach.

Index